VEGAN SOUPS
COOKBOOK

**DELICIOUS WINTER WARMING VEGAN SOUP RECIPES
TO SOOTHE YOUR SOUL**

Copyright © 2014 by Karen Braden
All Rights Reserved.

Disclaimer

Introduction

Going vegan is an oft-discussed topic. But why, do you think, are so many people going vegan and staying that way? It's not because vegan is the next "fad" diet. If it was, people would be in and out of the vegan lifestyle in an instant. Instead, going vegan offers essential lifestyle benefits that can truly alter everything about your outlook on life, your interior health, and your overall well-being. Vegan soups become natural elements of your vegan lifestyle, lending you essential minerals, vitamins, and nutrients in an enormous, steaming package of natural goodness.

Better understand the benefits of going vegan with the following information:

1. Vegan diets offer a reduced amount of saturated fats.

All meat and dairy products add saturated fats into your blood vessels and boost your risk of cardiovascular disease and heart attack. When you stop eating these dairy and meat products, you automatically reduce your intake of saturated fats and boost your heart health nearly instantly. You give your blood pressure a break and allow your body to calm itself down and deliver the appropriate amount of blood and oxygen to each of its cells without stress.

2. Vegan diets bring an appropriate level of potassium to your body.

Have you ever heard the concept of acidity in your body? Essentially, some of the things you eat boost the acid levels in your body and boost your risk of inflammation and certain diseases. In order to maintain a balanced pH in your system, you have to maintain a certain level of potassium in your cells. When you eat enough potassium through the vegan diet, your body is able to stimulate your kidneys to reduce your body's acid levels.

3. Vegan diets yield a healthier body mass index.

Your body requires an appropriate body mass index, or the appropriate ratio between your body weight and your body's skeletal size. When you are on the vegan diet, your body naturally loses the weight it's been carrying on the non-vegan diet. Your body becomes stronger, leaner, and pulsing with energy.

4. The vegan diet eliminates many environmental hazards.

When you follow a non-vegan diet, you are contributing to many environmental traumas throughout the world. For example: when you grow plants for your diet, you utilize far less resources than you do when you eat meat. Furthermore, you're becoming more conscious of animals and animal rights, which shows your compassion and appreciation for life. The vegan diet brings an essential awareness of your body, your weight, and your greater world. Go forth: eat vegetables, slurp "creamy" soup, and live a more natural existence.

TABLE OF CONTENTS

VEGAN
FAUX "CHEESE" AND CREAMY
SOUPS

"Cream" Based Carrot and Ginger Soup

Recipe Makes 8 Servings.

Nutritional Information: 206 calories, 22 grams carbohydrates, 10 grams fat, 7 grams protein.

Prep Time: 15 minutes.
Cook Time: 25 minutes.

Ingredients:
2 tsp. olive oil
1 diced onion
4 minced garlic cloves
1 ¾ pound diced carrots
6 cups vegetable broth
1 cup orange juice
2 ½ tbsp. grated ginger
1 cup soaked cashews
Salt and pepper to taste

Directions:
Begin by placing the cashews in a small bowl and then pouring water overtop. Allow the cashews to soak for two hours.

Heat olive oil in a large soup pot. Add onion and garlic to the olive oil and allow it to sauté for five minutes. Next, add orange juice, carrots, ginger, and the broth to the mixture. Stir the mixture well and allow it to boil. Next, reduce the heat to medium-low and allow it to simmer for twenty-five minutes. The vegetables should be tender. Turn off the stovetop and allow the soup to cool down for fifteen minutes.

Next, drain out the cashews and pour them in the blender. Add the rest of the cooked soup and blend the mixture together on low, gradually increasing it until it's able to handle all of the ingredients.

If you want, you can heat up the mixture a bit on the stove before serving the creamy soup. Enjoy!

Faux Cheese and Broccoli Soup

Recipe Makes 8 Servings.

Nutritional Information: 302 calories, 26 grams carbohydrates, 17 grams fat, 16 grams protein.

Prep Time: 15 minutes.
Cook time: 20 minutes.

Ingredients:

1 ½ tsp. olive oil
3 minced garlic cloves
1 diced onion
5 cups diced broccoli
1 cup diced celery
2 cups diced potatoes
4 cups vegetable broth
2 tbsp. nutritional yeast
½ tsp. cayenne pepper
Salt and pepper to taste

Faux Cheese Ingredients:

2 cups almond milk
1 tbsp. vegan butter spread
1 cup nutritional yeast

½ tsp. garlic powder

1 tbsp. Dijon mustard

½ tsp. onion powder

Salt and pepper

Directions:

Make the cheese sauce first so that you have it prepared for later.

Simply add the buttery spread into a saucepan and melt it over medium heat. Next, add about half of the almond milk and the flour into the saucepan and stir well until all the flour clumps are eliminated.

Next, add the rest of the milk into the saucepan, continuing to stir. Add the nutritional yeast and place the heat on medium-low.

Next, add all the remaining ingredients and continue to stir well. The sauce should begin to thicken as you whisk after about five minutes. After it's thick, remove the sauce from the heat.

Next, make your soup.

Heat the olive oil in a large soup pot. Add the garlic and the onion and sauté them for six minutes over medium-high heat.

Next, add the broccoli, celery, and the potatoes. Cook for an additional six minutes. Add the nutritional yeast, broth, and the cayenne pepper. Allow the mixture to simmer for twenty minutes to make the potatoes tender.

Bring the created soup together in a blender and blend the ingredients to your desired consistency. I like mine creamy with a few chunks in it, for example. After you've blended it, you can return the soup to its soup pot and add the faux cheese sauce. Add any salt and pepper you please to taste, and enjoy warm!

Creamy Celery and Spinach Herb Soup

Recipe Makes 6 Servings.

Nutritional Information: 144 calories, 10 grams carbohydrates, 10 grams fat, 4 grams protein.

Prep Time: 45 minutes.
Cook Time: 35 minutes.

Ingredients:
1 diced onion
2 tbsp. olive oil

4 minced garlic cloves

3 diced celery stalks

1 peeled and diced celeriac

4 cups vegetable stock

½ pound spinach

1 ½ tbsp. Dijon mustard

½ cup peas

½ cup chives

½ cup soaked cashews

Salt and pepper to taste

Directions:

Begin by bringing the cashews in a small bowl and pouring water overtop. Allow the cashews to sit overnight. Afterwards, remove the water and set the cashews to the side.

Next, pour the olive oil into a large soup pot. Add the garlic, onion, and the celery, and allow them to sauté or about ten minutes. Next, add the celeriac and the Dijon mustard. Cover the mixture and allow it to cook for about twelve minutes.

Next, add the vegetable stock. Bring the mixture up to a boil, uncovered, before next covering it and placing the heat on medium-low and allowing it to simmer for fifteen minutes. Next, add the spinach, peas, and the chives. Allow the mixture to simmer for an additional four minutes.

Next, remove the soup from the heat. Allow it to cool. Pour the soup into your blender along with the aforementioned cashews and blend the ingredients well. Season the soup with salt and pepper to taste, and then heat the soup once more— without boiling it. Serve the soup warm, and enjoy!

Creamy Pasta and Butternut Squash Soup

Recipe Makes 6 Servings.

Nutritional Information: 240 calories, 35 grams carbohydrates, 5 grams fat, 3 grams protein.

Prep Time: 10 minutes.
Cook Time: 30 minutes.

Ingredients:
4 minced garlic cloves
2 tbsp. olive oil
1 diced onion
1 chopped butternut squash
2 diced carrots
2 diced zucchini
7 cups vegetable stock
1 tsp. sage
1 tsp. oregano
2 cups rigate pasta
Salt and pepper to taste

Directions:

Begin by slicing and dicing the above ingredients.

Heat olive oil in a soup pot over medium. Add the onion and the garlic and allow them to sauté for five minutes. Next, add the butternut squash, zucchini, oregano, sage, and carrots. Salt and pepper the mixture and stir well. Allow it to cook for fifteen minutes before adding the stock. Allow the mixture to boil.

When the mixture begins to boil, place the heat on medium-low and allow it to simmer for twenty minutes. To the side, cook the pasta in two cups of boiling water until the pasta is al dente—about fifteen minutes, as well.

Next, pour the created soup in a blender and blend it until it's smooth. Add the pasta to the pureed mixture and season it as you please. Heat the soup up once more in the pot and serve the soup warm. Enjoy!

Summer Nights Creamed Corn Soup

Recipe Makes 6 Servings.

Nutritional Information: 303 calories, 33 grams carbohydrates, 18 grams fat, 7 grams protein.

Prep Time: 5 minutes
Cook Time: 20 minutes.

Ingredients:

1 ¼ cup coconut milk
2 tbsp. olive oil

3 ½ cups vegetable broth
2 sliced leeks
2 14-ounce cans of corn
½ tsp. chili powder
Salt and pepper to taste

Directions:

Begin by slicing and dicing the leeks. Next, place the olive oil in a large soup pot, and allow the leeks to cook in the oil over medium-high heat for three minutes.

Next, add the cans of corn—without the liquid, vegetable broth, and the coconut milk. Stir well, and allow the mixture to boil. After it begins to boil, turn the heat to medium-low and allow it to simmer for six minutes.

Remove the soup from the heat. Allow the soup to cool for about three minutes before blending the ingredients in a blender. Note that you might have to split up the soup to make it all fit.

Next, allow the soup to simmer once more on the stovetop before serving. Serve warm, and enjoy the delicious nature of this incredible, natural soup!

Traditional Thai Variety Vegetable Soup

Recipe Makes 12 Servings.

Nutritional Information: 350 calories, 31 grams carbohydrates, 24 grams fat, 13 grams protein.

Prep Time: 10 minutes.
Cook Time: 60 minutes.

Ingredients:
1 diced onion
2 diced red peppers
4 minced garlic cloves
1 ½ sliced carrots
1 15-ounce can of chickpeas
5 tbsp. olive oil
1 tsp. cumin
½ tsp. cayenne
3 cups diced tomatoes
1 cup peanut butter
1 ¼ cup coconut milk
Juice from 3 limes
1/3 cup vegetable broth
1/3 cup chopped cilantro

Directions:

Begin by bringing together peppers, onion, and garlic together in a large soup pot. Add the olive oil and cook the ingredients over medium-high heat for about seven minutes.

After seven minutes, add all the rest of the listed ingredients: carrots, chickpeas, cumin, cayenne, tomatoes, peanut butter, coconut milk, limes, and the broth. Do not add the cilantro yet. Bring the mixture to a simmer over medium-low heat and allow the mixture to cook for about one hour. Stir every few minutes.

Next, pour half of the above mixture into a blender and blend it well until you've created a smooth soup. Return the mixture back to the chunky part of the pot, add the cilantro for garnish, and enjoy!

Delicious Tomato Garlic Cream Soup

Recipe Makes 6 Servings.

Nutritional Information: 230 calories, 11 grams carbohydrates, 19 grams fat, 5 grams protein.

Prep Time: 15 minutes.
Cook Time: 20 minutes.

Ingredients:
3 ½ cups sliced roma tomatoes
2 minced garlic cloves

1 diced onion

1 tbsp. olive oil

1 14-ounce can coconut milk

4 cups vegetable broth

2 tsp. garam masala

3 tbsp. tomato paste

salt and pepper to taste

Directions:

Begin by bringing the olive oil, onion, garlic, and the tomatoes together in a large soup pot. Allow the mixture to sauté for twelve minutes, stirring occasionally. After these twelve minutes, add the tomato paste, the coconut milk, and the broth. Stir the ingredients well, and add the seasonings. Allow the mixture to come to a boil. Next, reduce the heat to medium-low and allow the mixture to simmer together for fifteen minutes.

Pour the mixture into a blender and blend the mixture, making it "creamy" with a bit of texture. Add the soup back to the soup pot to heat it up a bit without boiling it. Serve the soup warm, and enjoy!

VEGAN CHUNKY SOUPS

Super-Spiced Vegetables Soup

Recipe makes 8 Servings.

Nutritional Information: 175 calories, 18 grams carbohydrates, 3 grams fat, 4 grams protein.

Prep Time: 25 minutes.
Cook Time: 25 minutes.

Ingredients:
1 cup soaked cashews
1 tbsp. olive oil
5 cups vegetable broth

1 diced onion

4 minced garlic cloves

4 diced carrots

2 cups diced sweet potatoes

3 diced celery stalks

15 ounces diced tomatoes

15 ounces garbanzo beans

1 tsp. oregano

1 tsp. garlic powder

1 tsp. cayenne pepper

salt and pepper to taste

Directions:

Begin by placing the cashews in a small bowl and pouring water overtop. Allow them to soak for ten hours.

Next, drain the cashews and completely rinse them.

Pour the drained cashews into a blender with 1 cup of the vegetable broth. Blend the ingredients well.

Next, pour the olive oil in a large soup pot. Add the onion and the garlic and sauté them together in the oil for five minutes.

Next, add the rest of the vegetables to the soup along with the rest of the vegetable broth, the cashew broth, and the spices. Make sure not to add the beans yet. Stir the mixture well and then allow the mixture to come to a boil.

Afterwards, reduce the heat to a low temperature and allow the soup to simmer for twenty minutes. Stir every few minutes. The vegetables should become tender. About five minutes before it's finished cooking, add the complete can of beans.

Serve the soup warm, and enjoy!

Quinoa and Black Bean Soup

Recipe Makes 8 Servings.

Nutritional Information: 210 calories, 24 grams carbohydrates, 4 grams fat, 4 grams protein.

Prep Time: 20 minutes.
Cook Time: 30 minutes.

Ingredients:
1 ¼ cup uncooked and rinsed quinoa
4 minced garlic cloves
½ tbsp. olive oil
1 diced sweet potato
1 diced onion
1 diced jalapeno
1 tsp. chili powder
2 tsp. cumin
5 cups vegetable broth
1 tsp. coriander
15 ounces black beans
3 large handfuls spinach
½ tsp. cayenne pepper

Directions:

Begin by boiling the quinoa with 2 cups of water in a large pot. Allow the mixture to boil, and then reduce the heat to low. Cover the pot with a lid and allow the quinoa to simmer for twenty minutes. The quinoa should be appropriately fluffed. Remove the quinoa from the heat.

Next, heat the olive oil in a large soup pot. Sauté the onion and the garlic together in the pot over medium. Next, add the sweet potato and the jalapeno to the oil, as well, and sauté for eight more minutes.

Next, add all the spices and the vegetable broth. Allow the mixture to boil and then place the heat on low. Allow the mixture to simmer for twenty-five minutes until the sweet potatoes become soft.

After the twenty-five minutes, remove the soup from the heat and add the black beans, quinoa, spinach, and a bit of salt and pepper. Stir well, and serve warm. Enjoy!

Chunky Indian-Inspired Cabbage Soup

Recipe Makes 4 Servings.

Nutritional Information: 72 calories, 12 grams carbohydrates, 1 gram fat, 4 grams protein.

Prep Time: 10 minutes.
Cook Time: 20 minutes.

Ingredients:

1 ¼ pound chopped cabbage
2 ½ diced onions

2 ½ cups vegetable broth

3 minced garlic cloves

salt and pepper to taste

1 tsp. hot sauce or to taste

1 cup chopped cilantro

Directions:

Begin by preparing the cabbage, chopping it into smaller, bite-sized pieces. Add the onion, cabbage, broth, garlic, and the salt and pepper to a large soup pot. Allow the mixture to simmer for twenty minutes on medium-low, stirring every so often.

Next, pour half of the mixture into a blender and blend it until it's smooth. Add the mixture back to the chunky soup to bring a layered effect.

Next, add the hot sauce and the cilantro, and season to taste. Enjoy the soup warm!

Mexican Spiced Vegan Tortilla Soup

Recipe Makes 6 Servings.

Nutritional Information: 388 calories, 63 grams carbohydrates, 8 grams fat, 20 grams protein.

Prep Time: 15 minutes.
Cook Time: 35 minutes.

Ingredients:
1 ½ tbsp. olive oil
3 minced garlic cloves

2 diced onions

1 chopped zucchini

2 diced bell peppers

1 can of corn

3 ½ tbsp.. cumin

28 ounces tomatoes

3 cups vegetable broth

2 cans black beans

2 tbsp. chia seeds

salt and pepper to taste

2 flour tortillas

½ tbsp. olive oil

½ tsp. garlic powder

½ tsp. chili powder

Directions:

Begin by pouring olive oil, garlic, and onion into a large soup pot. Allow the mixture to sauté together for six minutes. During this time, preheat your broiler.

Next, dice the zucchini and the peppers. Remove and drain the corn from the can. Bring these ingredients into the soup pot and allow them to sauté for ten minutes.

Next, add the tomatoes, the broth, the cumin, and the chia seeds. Allow this mixture to simmer for thirty minutes on medium-low.

Next, create the tortilla strips by slicing the flour tortillas into small 2-inch long strips. Next, bring these into a small bowl and add the olive oil. Add the chili powder and the garlic powder and mix the ingredients with your hands. Place the tortilla strips on your baking sheet and broil them for three minutes. When they turn a golden color, remove them from the oven.

After the soup has simmered and the tortillas have baked, bring the soup into bowls and top it with the tortilla strips. Serve the soup, and enjoy!

Minestrone Mission Soup

Recipe Makes 4 Servings.

Nutritional Information: 388 calories, 61 grams carbohydrates, 8 grams fat, 17 grams protein.

Prep Time: 20 minutes.
Cook Time: 45 minutes.

Ingredients:
5 cups vegetable stock
1 cup chopped asparagus
2 tbsp. olive oil

1 ¼ cup broad beans

2 chopped leeks

2 cups sugar snaps

1 cup fine beans

2 sliced zucchinis

4 minced garlic cloves

½ cup spaghetti noodles

Directions:

Begin by heating the olive oil in a soup pot and then cooking the celery, leeks, and garlic together in the olive oil for ten minutes.

Next, add the zucchini, sugar snaps, both kinds of beans, and the asparagus. Place the lid on the pot and allow the mixture to heat together or ten minutes, stirring occasionally.

Next, add the vegetable broth and allow the mixture to boil. Once it begins the boiling process, place the heat on medium-low and add some salt and pepper. Allow the mixture to simmer for fifteen minutes. Next, add the spaghetti noodles and allow the mixture to simmer for another ten minutes. The spaghetti noodles should be al dente.

Next, serve the mixture warm with a bit of vegan pesto overtop, and enjoy!

Stick-to-Your-Bones Slow Cooker Split Pea Soup

Recipe Makes 8 Servings.

Nutritional Information: 224 calories, 40 grams carbohydrates, 1 gram fat, 13 grams protein.

Prep Time: 10 minutes.
Cook Time: 240 minutes.

Ingredients:
2 ¼ cup green split peas
7 cups vegetable broth

2 chopped celery stalks
2 chopped potatoes
1 diced onion
2 sliced carrots
3 minced garlic cloves
1 tsp. cumin
1 tsp. mustard seeds
1 tsp. sage
½ tsp. cumin
2 bay leaves
salt and pepper to taste

Directions:
Bring all the above ingredients together into a slow cooker, making sure to stir as you administer each ingredient. Afterwards, cover the slow cooker and cook the soup on LOW for about four hours. The peas should be soft. Season the soup to taste, and enjoy warm!

Chunky Edamame and Buckwheat Groat Stew

Recipe Makes 10 servings.

Nutritional Information: 150 calories, 24 grams carbohydrates, 3 grams fat, 6 grams protein.

Prep Time: 15 minutes.
Cook Time: 30 minutes.

Ingredients:
2 diced onions
1 ½ tbsp. olive oil
4 minced garlic cloves
1 tsp. coriander
1 tsp. cinnamon
2 ½ diced zucchini
1 diced red pepper
1 diced yellow pepper
4 diced carrots
5 cups vegetable broth
½ cup raw buckwheat groats
28 ounces diced tomatoes
½ cup raw pearled barley
2 tbsp. lemon juice

¾ cup frozen Edamame

1 tbsp. red pepper flakes

salt and pepper to taste

Directions:

Begin by bringing together the olive oil, the onion, and the garlic in a large soup pot. Allow this mixture to heat for ten minutes on medium-high, stirring occasionally.

At this time, add the cinnamon and the coriander. Stir well and allow this to cook for three more minutes. Next, add the carrots, the peppers, and the zucchini and allow the mixture to cook for six additional minutes.

Next, add the ounces of tomatoes, Edamame, broth, buckwheat, and barley. Allow this mixture to simmer on medium-low or about twenty-five minutes. Stir occasionally. If it loses water, you can continue to add it a bit at a time to keep it fresh and lively.

After that twenty-five minutes, toss in the lemon juice and all the other ingredients.

Stir well and allow it to heat for an additional three minutes. Next, serve the stew warm, and enjoy!

Bamboo and Mushroom Chinese-Inspired Soup

Recipe Makes 6 Servings.

Nutritional Information: 106 calories, 6 grams carbohydrates, 6 grams fat, 7 grams protein.

Prep Time: 10 minutes.
Cook Time: 25 minutes.

Ingredients:
5 ½ cups vegetable broth
2 ½ cups sliced mushrooms
1 10-ounce can water chestnuts
1 10-ounce can bamboo shoots
3 tbsp. soy sauce
1 tsp. hot sauce
2 ½ tbsp. vinegar
4 minced garlic cloves
2 tbsp. chili oil
½ cup sliced green onions

Directions:
Begin by pouring the vegetable broth into a large soup pot. Add the mushrooms,

chestnuts, bamboo shoots, soy sauce, hot sauce, vinegar, garlic cloves, and chili oil, and allow the mixture to simmer at medium for twenty minutes.

After twenty minutes, add the green onions, and allow the mixture to simmer for an additional five minutes. Season the mixture to taste, adding additional hot sauce, vinegar, or soy sauce. Stir well after each addition.

Enjoy the soup warm, and enjoy!

Chunky Thai Coconut Soup

Recipe Makes 6 Servings.

Nutritional Information: 224 calories, 14 grams fat, 7 grams protein.

Prep Time: 15 minutes.
Cook Time: 15 minutes.

Ingredients:
2 minced garlic cloves
2 tbsp. olive oil
1 tbsp. brown sugar
1/3 cup red curry paste

3 cups vegetable broth

2 13-ounce cans coconut milk

1/3 cup peeled ginger

1/3 cup lime juice

4 sliced carrots

8 ounces green beans

14 ounces cubed tofu

1 cup chopped cilantro

Directions:

Begin by pouring the olive oil into a large soup pot. Heat the garlic in the olive oil for about one minute on medium-high heat. Next, add the red curry paste and sauté for an additional minute, stirring all the time. Toss in the brown sugar and cook for another minute.

Next, add the vegetable broth, coconut milk, lime juice, ginger, and soy sauce to the soup pot. Stir well and place the heat on low. Cover the mixture and allow it to cook for sixty minutes. Next, add the carrots. Cook for an additional ten minutes. Toss in the green beans and cook for another five minutes. The carrots and the beans should be a bit tender.

Afterwards, add the tofu to the soup pot and cook for an additional three minutes. Serve warm with the chopped cilantro overtop. Enjoy!

Butter Bean and Green Soup

Recipe Makes 6 Servings.

Nutritional Information: 190 calories, 28 grams carbohydrates, 4 grams fat, 5 grams protein.

Prep Time: 15 minutes.
Cook Time: 25 minutes.

Ingredients:
30 ounces butter beans
2 tbsp. olive oil
1 diced onion
4 minced garlic cloves
2 tbsp. tomato paste
2 diced carrots
2 diced celery stalks
¾ pound chopped kale
2 tsp. Italian herbs
5 cups vegetable stock
15 ounces diced tomatoes
Salt and pepper to taste

Directions:

Begin by heating olive oil in a large soup pot. Add the onion and the garlic first, allowing them to sauté for six minutes. Next, add the carrot, celery, and the herbs and stir well for about five minutes.

Next, add the tomato paste to the mix and stir for about two minutes. Next, add the broth, beans, chopped tomatoes, and chopped kale. Allow this mixture to boil on medium-high. When it begins to boil, place the heat on low and cover the pot. Allow the mixture to simmer for twenty minutes.

Afterwards, administer a bit of salt and pepper and serve the soup warm. Enjoy!

VEGAN
VEGAN LENTIL-BASED SOUPS
SOUPS

Chunky Lentil and Kale Soup

Recipe Makes 8 servings.

Nutritional Information: 175 calories, 19 grams carbohydrates, 2 grams fat, 3 grams protein.

Prep Time: 20 minutes.
Cook Time: 25 minutes.

Ingredients:

1 tsp. olive oil
1 diced onion
3 minced garlic cloves
4 diced celery stalks
½ tsp. cumin
3 tsp. chili powder
½ tsp. paprika
5 cups vegetable broth
15 ounces diced tomatoes
1 cup rinsed lentils
3 cups kale

Directions:

Begin by slicing and dicing all the above ingredients. Next, bring together oil, garlic, and the onion in your large soup pot. Allow them to sauté for six minutes. Next, add the celery and sauté for two more minutes.

Add all the spices to the mixture and stir well. Next, add the broth, tomatoes, and the lentils. Continue to stir and then allow the mixture to boil. Place the heat on medium-low and then allow the mixture to simmer—without a top on the pot—for twenty-five minutes.

Add the kale to the mixture, salt and pepper as you please, and stir well. Serve warm, and enjoy!

Super Lentil and Garlic Chunked Soup

Recipe Makes 5 Servings.

Nutritional Information: 210 calories, 25 grams carbohydrates, 6 grams fat, 4 grams protein.

Prep Time: 15 minutes.
Cook Time: 60 minutes.

Ingredients:
1 diced onion
2 tsp. olive oil
5 minced garlic cloves
½ tsp. coriander
¾ cup diced celery
½ tsp. cinnamon
1 tsp. cumin
6 cups vegetable broth
¾ cup black lentils
½ cup red lentils
¾ cup green lentils
Salt and pepper to taste

Directions:

Begin by pouring oil into a large soup pot. Place the heat on medium-high and allow the onion and the garlic to sauté for eight minutes.

Next, add the celery and continue to sauté for three minutes. Add all of the spices and stir well, keeping the heat on medium-high.

Next, add the various types of lentils: the red, the green, and the black. Stir well, and add the broth. Place the heat on high and allow the mixture to boil. When it begins to boil, cover the mixture and place the heat on low. Allow the soup to cook for about fifty minutes beneath the cover. After fifty minutes, pour ¼ of the soup into a blender and blend it well to create a more soup-like consistency throughout. Add the blended soup to the chunky soup, and serve warm. Add salt and pepper as needed.

Lentil and Curried Squash Soup

Recipe Makes 5 Servings.

Nutritional Information: 160 calories, 27 grams carbohydrates, 4 grams fat, 4 grams protein.

Prep Time: 15 minutes.
Cook Time: 20 minutes.

Ingredients:
1 diced onion
1 ½ tsp. olive oil
1 ½ tbsp. curry powder

4 minced garlic cloves

1 ¼ cup red lentils

4 cups vegetable broth

1 cup diced broccoli

3 ½ cups pre-cooked butternut squash cubes

½ tsp. ginger

salt and pepper to taste

Directions:

Begin by pouring the olive oil into a large soup pot. Add the minced garlic and the onion to the olive oil, and sauté them together for six minutes over medium heat.

Next, add the curry powder. Stir well for a few minutes, and then add both the lentils and the broth. Allow the mixture to come to a boil. Then, reduce the head to low and cook for fifteen minutes, stirring occasionally.

Afterwards, add the diced broccoli and the pre-baked butternut squash to the soup. Cook this mixture for another ten minutes, stirring occasionally. Add salt, pepper, and ginger, and stir well. Serve warm, and enjoy!

Lentil Indian Broccoli Dal Soup

Recipe Makes 8 Servings.

Nutritional Information: 340 calories, 24 grams carbohydrates, 23 grams fat, 12 grams protein.

Prep Time: 15 minutes.
Cook Time: 35 minutes.

Ingredients:
1 cup uncooked red lentils
1 diced onion
2 tsp. mustard seeds
½ tsp. cumin
2 tbsp. olive oil
5 cups diced broccoli
5 cups vegetable broth
2 ½ cups almond milk
2 tbsp. lemon juice
1 tsp. Garam Masala
1 tsp. red pepper flakes
½ tsp. turmeric
Salt and pepper to taste

Directions:

Begin by pouring oil into a large stove pot. Next, add onion, lentils, mustard seeds, and the cumin, and cook the mixture, stirring occasionally, for about ten minutes. the mustard seeds should pop.

Next, add the broccoli pieces to the food processor to create a fine "meal."

Pour the broccoli and the vegetable broth into the large soup pot and stir. Cover the mixture and allow the mixture to simmer for twenty minutes.

After these twenty minutes have passed, add the lemon juice, almond milk, garam masala, red pepper flakes, and any salt and pepper to taste. Stir well and cook for an additional eight minutes, stirring occasionally. Serve the soup warm, and enjoy!

Simple Winter's Day Carrot and Lentil Soup

Recipe Makes 4 Servings.

Nutritional Information: 230 calories, 33 grams carbohydrates, 3 grams fat, 18 grams protein.

Prep Time: 5 minutes.
Cook Time: 50 minutes.

Ingredients:
2 tsp. olive oil
1 sliced carrot

2 diced onions
4 ½ cups vegetable broth
1 ¼ cup dried lentils
½ tsp. dried thyme
3 bay leaves
salt and pepper to taste
½ tbsp. lemon juice

Directions:

Begin by bringing the carrots and the onions together with the olive oil in a large soup pot. Sauté for five minutes.

Next, add the lentils, vegetable broth, thyme, bay leaves, and the salt and pepper. Stir well, and place the heat on medium-low. Cover the mixture and allow it to simmer for forty-five minutes.

Take the bay leaves out of the soup pot and add the lemon juice. Serve the lentil soup warm, and enjoy!

VEGAN

VEGAN COLD SOUPS

SOUPS

Avocado and Lime Creamy Cold Soup

Recipe Makes 4 Servings.

Nutritional Information: 127 calories, 10 grams carbohydrates, 10 grams fat, 2 grams protein.

Prep Time: 10 minutes.
Chill Time: 2 hours.

Ingredients:
2 cucumbers
1 avocado

2 tbsp. lime juice

1 tsp. salt

5 tbsp. parsley

Directions:

Begin by peeling the cucumbers and taking the meat out of the avocado. Then, add the ingredients together into a food processor and process the ingredients until they're completely smooth. Add a bit of salt and pepper.

Pour the blended soup in a container and allow it to chill in the refrigerator for two hours. Afterwards, serve, and enjoy!

Devour Walnut Chilled Soup

Recipe Makes 8 Servings.

Nutritional Information: 320 calories, 10 grams carbohydrates, 30 grams fat, 10 grams protein.

Prep Time: 10 minutes.
Cook Time: 30 minutes.

Ingredients:
2 cups diced walnuts
1 cup soaked cashews
2 tbsp. olive oil

4 diced celery Sticks
3 diced shallots
4 cups vegetable stock
salt and pepper

Directions:

Begin by bringing the cashews together in a small bowl and pouring water overtop of them. Allow the cashews to sit in the water for at least six hours. Next, pour out the water and set them to the side.

Next, heat up the olive oil in your soup pot. Add the shallots and the celery and stir well. Next, add the diced walnuts and allow them to sauté for five additional minutes.

Add the vegetable stock to the soup pot and allow it to boil. Cover the pot and allow it to simmer for fifteen minutes.

Next, take the soup off the heat. Puree this mixture with the aforementioned cashews in a blender of a food processor. Season the soup with salt and pepper. Then, chill the soup in the refrigerator for ten hours, and enjoy cold. This soup is essential for backyard summer dinners!

French Potato "Vichyssoise" Soup

Recipe Makes 4 Servings.

Nutritional Information: 280 calories, 26 grams carbohydrates, 18 grams fat, 8 grams protein.

Prep Time: 15 minutes.
Chill Time: 2 hours.

Ingredients:
2 ½ tbsp. olive oil
3 sliced leeks

1 diced onion

3 ½ cups vegetable broth

1 sliced and diced potato

½ cup soaked cashews

½ tsp. nutmeg

Salt and pepper to taste

Directions:

A few hours before you get started, pour the cashews into a small bowl and top the cashews with water. Allow the cashews to soak for six hours before draining them and using them in the soup recipe.

Begin by slicing the leeks and bringing leeks, onion, and the olive oil together in a large soup pot. Allow the mixture to heat on medium-high heat for ten minutes.

Next, add the vegetable broth and the diced potatoes, allowing the mixture to simmer on medium heat until the potatoes are tender.

Remove the soup from the heat and allow the soup to cool. Bring this soup together with the aforementioned drained cashews. Blend this mixture together in a blender. Note that you might have to separate the soup a few times to make everything fit.

Add the nutmeg, the salt and the pepper, and season the soup to taste.

Place the soup in the refrigerator and allow it to chill for at least two hours. Enjoy your soup chilled.

Humming Citrus Summertime Soup

Recipe Makes 6 Servings.

Nutritional Information: 171 calories, 11 grams carbohydrates, 13 grams fat, 3 grams protein.

Prep Time: 10 minutes.
Chill Time: 2 hours.

Ingredients:
2 avocadoes
2 cups vegetable stock
Juice from 1 grapefruit
2 tbsp. agave nectar
2 minced garlic cloves
Salt and pepper to taste

Directions:
Begin by removing the avocado meat from the greater shell. Next, bring together the avocado meat, vegetable stock, grapefruit juice, agave nectar, garlic cloves, and the salt and pepper together in a food processor. Blend the ingredients

well to achieve a smooth consistency. Add salt and pepper and taste the mixture. Place the soup in the refrigerator when satisfied and allow the soup to chill for two

hours prior to serving. Enjoy!

VEGAN
VEGAN DESSERT SOUPS
SOUPS

Frothy Chocolate and Coconut Macaroon Soup

Recipe Makes 4 Servings.

Nutritional Information: 282 calories, 16 grams carbohydrates, 24 grams fat, 3 grams protein.

Prep Time: 5 minutes.
Cook Time: 10 minutes.

Ingredients:
14 ounce can of coconut milk
1/3 cup Date sugar
2 tsp. amaretto
2 ½ tbsp. cocoa powder
1 tsp. corn starch
1 tsp. vanilla

Directions:
Begin by mixing together date sugar, cocoa powder, and the cornstarch to the side in a small bowl.

Next, pour the coconut milk, amaretto, and the vanilla into a small saucepan and set the heat to medium. Allow the mixture to boil for just a moment before pouring in the dry ingredients and stirring well. Allow the mixture to boil once more before turning the heat to low and allowing it to simmer for just five minutes, stirring occasionally. Serve this dessert warm, and enjoy!

African Carrot Zest Soup

Recipe Makes 6 Servings.

Nutritional Information: 127 calories, 28 grams carbohydrates, 1 gram fat, 2 grams protein.

Prep Time: 25 minutes.
Cook Time: 0 minutes.

Ingredients:
3 ½ cups orange juice
½ peeled cucumber
2 cups grated carrots

1 tbsp. date sugar

½ tsp. cinnamon

Directions:

Begin by grating your carrots ad your cucumbers. Place them together in a large bowl. Add the orange juice, sugar, and the cinnamon. Pour this mixture into the food processor or the blender and blend it together until it's blended but still a bit chunky. Then, pour the soup back into a sealable container and chill the soup for at least two hours before serving. Enjoy!

Very Cherry Summer Dessert Soup

Recipe Makes 4 Servings.

Nutritional Information: 240 calories, 50 grams carbohydrates, 0 grams fat, 1 gram protein.

Prep Time: 5 minutes.
Cook Time: 25 minutes.

Ingredients:
1 pound fresh or canned cherries
3 cloves
1 cinnamon stick
1/3 cup agave nectar
Juice from a half a lemon
1/3 cup sugar
1 cup red wine
1 cup water

Directions:
Begin by bringing all the cherries together in a big soup pot. Next, add the sugar overtop the cherries and break the cinnamon stick apart over both

ingredients. Add the cloves, as well. Stir for a moment, and then add the rest of the ingredients.

Place the stovetop to medium-high and allow the mixture to come to a boil. After it boils for about thirty seconds, place the heat on low and allow the mixture to simmer, covered, for twenty minutes. The cherries should be soft to the touch. Taste the soup and add any lemon juice or sugar, if it needs it. Serve the soup warm and enjoy!

Super-Easy Chilled Mango Soup

Recipe Makes 6 Servings.

Nutritional Information: 137 calories, 33 grams carbohydrates, 0 grams fat, 0 grams protein.

Prep Time: 10 minutes.
Chill Time: 2 hours

Ingredients:
2 peeled and diced mangoes
1 cup mango juice
2 tsp. agave nectar

Juice from 1 lime

Directions:
Begin by peeling and dicing the mangoes. Place the juice, mangoes, agave, and the lime juice together in a food processor or a blender. Blend the ingredients well until you reach a smooth consistency. If the consistency is too thick, you can add a little extra mango juice, if desired.

Next, chill the created mango soup for about two hours prior to serving. Enjoy with a fruit garnish!

Vegan Strawberry Vanilla Soup

Recipe Makes 6 Servings.

Nutritional Information: 86 calories, 17 grams carbohydrates, 1 gram fat, 2 grams protein.

Prep Time: 25 minutes.
Cook Time: 0 minutes.

Ingredients:
4 cups sliced strawberries
1 cup vegan vanilla yogurt

1 ¼ cup sparkling water

1 tsp. vanilla

½ tbsp. caster sugar

Directions:

Begin by bringing 3 and a half cups of strawberries, all the vegan yogurt, and the vanilla together in a blender. Blend the ingredients well until they're smooth. Chill this mixture in the fridge for three hours.

Next, create the "sauce" on top by mixing the sugar and the strawberries in a small saucepan. Cook them together over medium high heat until the sauce begins to thicken. This should take about seven minutes. Afterwards, allow the mixture to cool, pour it into a blender, and blend it well. Chill the sauce in the fridge for another 1.5 hours.

When you wish to serve the soup, add the sparkling water. Next, stir well, portion the soup into different bowls, and add the sauce overtop. Enjoy!

Conclusion

The Vegan Diet administers all the appropriate nutrients, vitamins, and minerals your body needs to strip you of your weight, boost you with ripe amounts of energy, and supercharge your health. When you choose to make these vegan soups, you are fueling yourself with a better, more balanced life. You are becoming a conscious consumer, and you are creating warmth and health in every cell of your body. Enjoy your newfound lifestyle, and understand why the vegan world is not retreating fast. All you need is a soup pot, a few vegetables, and an appetite to conquer this vegan soup revolution. Enjoy the winter months ahead!

Made in the USA
San Bernardino, CA
08 November 2017